See What God Can Do

Inspiration for Your Journey

Jean P. Good

TEACH Services, Inc.
P U B L I S H I N G
www.TEACHServices.com • (800) 367-1844

Copyright © 2020 Jean P. Good
Copyright © 2020 TEACH Services, Inc.
ISBN-13: 978-1-4796-1172-0 (Paperback)
ISBN-13: 978-1-4796-1173-7 (ePub)
Library of Congress Control Number: 2020906854

All scripture quotations, unless otherwise indicated, are taken from the King James Version®. Public Domain

Scripture quotations marked NKJV are taken from the New King James Version®. Copyright © 1982 by Thomas Nelson. Used by permission. All rights reserved.

Published by

TEACH Services, Inc.
P U B L I S H I N G
www.TEACHServices.com • (800) 367-1844

Dedication

To my five sons: Ian, Irvin, Isaac, Isaiah, and Simeon:

I love each of you with all of my heart, and my one desire is for you to come to know the God of Abraham, Isaac, Jacob, and Mom, whom to know is life eternal (see John 17:3). As you take this walk down memory lane, may you be reminded again and again of God's undying love and faithfulness to you.

And to the memory of my good friend and colleague of thirty-four years, Robert Moses, who encouraged me greatly and would always say, "Jean, you're better than you think you are." I wish he were here to witness the fruit of his encouragement.

Table of Contents

Foreword

Sometimes the most magnificent things happen through the most ordinary events, and that is what Jean Good shows us through this book of personal experiences. Jean is a person who has devoted herself to literature ministry, an often misunderstood and unappreciated work. Literature evangelists go into the homes of people with no idea of what they will find when they enter the home. It is a daunting and occasionally dangerous work that requires a faith that moves mountains, a courage that refuses to be cowered by fear, and a love that never fails. There was a time when literature evangelists were a large and vital part of the outreach ministry of the Seventh-day Adventist Church, but over the years, fewer and fewer people have responded to the call to engage in this most personal of ministries. It is not a prestigious ministry, the pay is neither abundant nor predictable, and fewer people are attracted to it, but Jean Good accepted the call and has never looked back.

Each episode in this narrative represents a unique adventure of faith and a testimony of the goodness of God. What is most remarkable is the courage Jean displays with the recitation of her personal struggles and how God has worked in her life. The authenticity of her experiences is encouraging to anyone who is struggling financially, spiritually, or emotionally.

At the end of the day, this is a work of great optimism, which proves that despite the problems a person may face, God can and will change things for the better, and Jean is exhibit A. A positive, personable, and sensitive woman, her faith and commitment to helping people to change for the better belies the suffering she has experienced, and the burdens she still carries for those who are close to her. Thankfully, she is still excited about sharing God's work with others. Those of us who are privileged to know and work with Jean know that in her quiet, unobtrusive way, she continues to bless people one by one, and we are among the ones who are blessed.

Norman K. Miles Sr., PhD
Senior Pastor
Trinity Temple Seventh-day Adventist Church
Newark, New Jersey

Acknowledgments

My colleague, Robert Moses used to say, "If you ever see a turtle sitting on top of a fence, you can be sure of one thing. It didn't get there by itself." Well, I am that turtle. I did not arrive at this point on my own, because Jesus says in John 15:5, "for without me ye can do nothing." So first and without fail, I want to thank my Lord and Savior who has allowed me the privilege of being a co-laborer with Him in the salvation of souls and blessing me with the incredible experiences that are recorded in this book. All glory, honor, and praise go to Jesus.

There are many people, from family to friends to co-workers, who have encouraged me over the years to write out my experiences. To you, I say thank you. This book is the fruit that has blossomed from the seeds of encouragement and confidence that you have sown into my life.

A very special and heartfelt thank you to Pastor Richard P. Campbell, who took the time out of his busy schedule to gather and edit my manuscript. Pastor Campbell said something to me one evening that stuck in my mind like a sticky note, "Jean, your lifework will not be complete until you put pen to paper. You have a story to tell, and people need to hear it." Thank you for encouraging and motivating me to actually begin writing, and for patiently guiding me through this process. Your wisdom and counsel have been invaluable. I will never be able to repay you for what you have done, but may the Lord reward you tenfold for your kindness towards me.

A special thank you to Dr. Norman Miles for taking the time out of his hectic schedule to read my manuscript and write the foreword for my book. Thank you for your kind words of endorsement and affirmation. And thank you to the entire Northern New Jersey Ministerium of pastors for the awesome support that you have given me and my ministry through the years. This has got to be the best ministerium in North America.

And to all who have ever prayed a prayer, spoken a word, or done a deed of kindness with me in mind, this grateful thank you is for you.

Introduction: Who is Jean Good?

If I were asked to describe myself in only one word, I could not. It would have to be two words—loyal and compassionate, for they both equally paint an accurate picture of who I am. Loyalty is the brush, and compassion is the stroke of paint upon my canvas.

I tend to be very loyal to my commitments, whether they be large or small. I remember when I was a teenager, around fifteen or sixteen, a strange feeling came over me that I could not explain or understand. I was overcome with a sense that whatever I endeavored to do in life would require my all. Over the years, this earlier revelation has come to pass, for I try to give 100 percent while seeking to keep my word, and that dependability is an important part of who I am.

I also consider myself a very compassionate person. My nature is quite sensitive, and it pains me to see suffering in any form, whether animal or human. I am attracted to people who are hurting like a magnet to metal, and I have been this way as far back as I can remember. I am usually the one to bring a sense of calmness and stability to chaotic situations.

Newark, New Jersey, is the city of my birth and upbringing. I was reared by my mother in a single-parent household. She was a disciplinarian and a very hard worker who provided for my brother and me as best she could, but she was also emotionally distant, so we did not have the proverbial mother-daughter relationship.

At the tender age of thirteen, I was raped at knifepoint, resulting in the birth of my first child. Paralyzed with fear from being threatened with harm to myself and my family if I told anyone, I kept silent and carried this heavy weight for seven and a half months. No one knew I was pregnant until six weeks before I gave birth! This was just one of many traumatic events to follow in my life, but God has delivered me from them all.

I mention this specific experience for two reasons. First, because there are so many young girls and women who have been violated in this way, and are carrying around a backpack filled with shame, guilt, self-hatred, and a feeling of worthlessness. They are suffering in silence and isolation with no one to talk to about their emotional pain. I remember some years ago, after sharing my testimony at a certain church, an elderly lady in her seventies came up to me with tears in her eyes and said, "Thank you for sharing." She leaned over and whispered in my ear that she, too, had been raped when she was in her early twenties and had kept this dark secret for more than fifty years! I was the first person with whom she had felt comfortable enough to tell. She said that she felt as though a heavy burden had been lifted from her shoulders.

Reader, I want to assure you that if you or someone you know has been through this terrible ordeal, God is able to restore your dignity, your self-respect, and whatever else the devil has tried to snatch from you. Yes, I still have scars, but they are only visible reminders of Jeremiah 30:17, "For I will restore health unto thee, and I will heal thee of thy wounds, saith the Lord."

Secondly, I relate this experience because, more than any other, it has had a profound impact on how I express myself verbally. I learned silence at an early age and still tend to keep my true feelings hidden. Rarely does anyone catch more than a glimpse into the inner world of Jean Good, although I must admit that I am improving in this area of my life. A good friend of mine would often tell me that I was the most private-outgoing person they had ever met.

The Lord has gifted me with the ability to reach out to those who are hurting and to touch their lives on a deep emotional level. I try to give to others what I desire for myself. That's the golden rule, right? My daily prayer is that God will let me be a rainbow in someone else's cloud.

I am the mother of five adult sons, whom I love dearly, and carry upon my heart as the high priest wore the names of the twelve tribes of the children of Israel upon his breastplate. The Lord has blessed me to see three generations, with twelve grandchildren and two adorable great-grandsons.

In 1980, I became a Christian and was baptized by Elder Alvin M. Kibble into the fellowship of the Trinity Temple Seventh-day Adventist Church in Newark. God has blessed me abundantly and above measure; hence, my reason and motivation for writing this book. I have always enjoyed writing, which has become very therapeutic for me. It is an avenue whereby I can express my thoughts and feelings. I have written many poems, but this is my first published work. I am certain that it is long overdue, for God has done many miraculous things in my life, especially through the literature evangelism ministry, my life-work for over thirty-six years.

After graduating from high school, I attended Rutgers University in Newark for two years with the aspiration of one day becoming a doctor, but what I soon learned was the truth of Proverbs 16:9, "A man's heart plans his way, but the Lord directs his steps" (NKJV). Yes, the Lord had other plans for my life. In the summer of 1982, He called me into full-time ministry as a literature evangelist, spreading the gospel through the distribution of

Bible-based literature. This has been my sole occupation since that time.

It is a great work and has afforded me many opportunities to walk in the footprints of Jesus and minister to people by following His method of evangelism. In the book *Ministry of Healing*, it says, "The Saviour mingled with men as one who desired their good. He showed His sympathy for them, ministered to their needs, and won their confidence. Then he bade them, 'Follow Me'" (p. 143). This is true evangelism, for as is often said, "No one cares how much you know until they know how much you care."

So, what would I like for you as the reader to take away from this book? Only one thing—that *God is faithful*. He can be trusted to do exactly what He said He would do. His promises are sure. If, after reading the last chapter, you come to the same conclusion, then the intent of the author will have been realized.

Blessings to you,
Jean Good

1
A Blind Blessing

I lived and worked in Baltimore, Maryland, for eighteen years as a literature evangelist. During those years God blessed me in miraculous ways. One day while out knocking on doors, I met a blind lady. She invited me to come in, and I began to share with her the service that I was providing through Bible-based literature. She sat on the edge of her seat and listened very intently to my presentation.

I introduced her to a set of health books along with a wonderful Bible study book called *Ask the Prophets* by the late Dr. E. E. Cleveland. She said that she really liked the book; however, she wouldn't be able to read it because she was blind. I asked her if she had someone, maybe a family member, who could read to her. She said that she had a daughter whom she didn't see very often. She also had a nurse who came to help her, but the nurse was legally blind!

"Oh, that Bible study book sounds so interesting, I've just got to have it," she exclaimed. Then she said something that just blew my mind. "I'll purchase it on one condition."

I said, "What's that?"

She responded, "If you will come and read it to me!" I gladly accepted the condition. She purchased *Ask the Prophets*, and once a week, I would go to her home and read to her. As she listened, she would say, "Praise the Lord," and, "Thank You, Jesus."

I did this for about a month, but one day when I came to her home, she reported that she had heard from her daughter, and she would be reading to her from now on. She thanked me over and over again for helping her, and I left there feeling as though I had been in the very presence of God. It was one of the most awesome and humbling experiences that I have ever had.

I felt like Isaiah 42:6–7 had been fulfilled to me: "I the Lord have called thee in righteousness, and will hold thine hand, and will keep thee, and give thee for a covenant of the people, for a light of the Gentiles; to open the blind eyes, to bring out the prisoners from the prison, and them that are in darkness out of the prison house." What an honor and a privilege to be able to minister and be of service to one of God's children. It doesn't get any better than that!

2

The Blessing of a Second Chance

Baltimore is well-known for its row houses. I lived in one and had a remarkable experience that I will never forget. It was a hot and uncomfortable summer evening as I lay in my bed, trying to sleep. The more that I tried, the more that sleep seemed to evade me. Not only was I bothered by the heat and humidity, but to make matters worse, I could hear the conversation of my next-door neighbor. That's one of the downsides of living in a row house. The walls seem to be paper-thin.

As I lay there in frustration, trying to tune out the distraction, something caught my ear. My neighbor's boyfriend was trying to wake her up. He began yelling and pleading for her not to pass out. At that moment, I realized that she had overdosed on drugs. I lay there in disbelief as I heard his desperate attempts to awaken her. Immediately, I began to pray that the Lord would intervene on her behalf and spare her life. My prayer was not only for her, but for myself as well, that God would give me another opportunity because I knew that I had not witnessed to her about the love of God. I said, "Lord, please spare her life so that I can tell her about you."

Praise God! He heard my plea, and after a while, she came around.

> *You never know if your voice will be the last sound that they will hear.*

The very next day, I knocked on her door and began to witness and minister to her. As I showed her some literature, she told me that she wanted to get *The Bible Story* for her children because her mother had purchased them for her and her siblings when she was a little girl. As I inquired further, I discovered that Robert Moses, who was my district publishing leader at the time, was the one who had sold her mother *The Bible Story* when she was about eight years old.

What a mighty God we serve! "He is able to save them to the uttermost that come unto God by him, seeing he ever liveth to make intercession for them" (Heb. 7:25).

She told me that she had decided to get some help for her drug addiction. I was able to pray with her and leave some religious literature, and she thanked me for taking the time to come to her and show my concern. This experience has taught me to be more attentive and listen to the voice of the Holy Spirit when He impresses me to speak to someone. You never know if your voice will be the last sound that they will hear. Thank God for second chances, both hers and mine!

3

Blessed by Rudy
and Trudy

One December day, while I was knocking on doors in Baltimore, Maryland, I met a man who was working on his car. His name was Rudy. I introduced him to the *Bible Reference Library*. As I went through my presentation, he recognized one of the books and told me that a few years prior, he had purchased *Prophets and Kings* from someone who had come to his home. He expressed an interest in the rest of the set, and he gave me a down payment. He asked if he should mail in the remaining payments, but I told him that I lived only a few blocks from him and would pick them up. I had prayer with him and went home rejoicing about the experience, not knowing that the Lord had additional blessings in store for me.

About a week later, someone knocked at my door. It was Rudy. He said that he had shared with his wife, Trudy, how much of a blessing I had been to him by sharing the books and praying for him. He said that he and his wife would like to invite my family and me to join them for Christmas dinner as a token of their appreciation. I was really taken aback by this gesture of kindness. After praying about it, I decided to accept the invitation. It was one of the most beautiful and meaningful Christmases that I have ever spent.

When my two young sons and I arrived at their home, we were cordially welcomed and were seated to enjoy a delicious dinner. I got a chance to meet his wife, Trudy, and their two children. They even went as far as to give Christmas gifts to my children and me. As Rudy, Trudy, and I talked about the goodness of the Lord, they told me how grateful they were that I had come to their home and shared such wonderful books. Before I left, we all had prayer together, and as my children and I returned home, we basked in the warmth of God's love and His amazing grace. This was one of my most memorable experiences. I'll be looking for Rudy and Trudy on that great day when, once again, I'll sit with them around a "welcome table."

4

An "Oodles of Noodles" Blessing, Part 1

W hen I joined the church in 1980, three biblical principles resounded from the pulpit on a systematic basis. The first one was health reform (see 1 Cor. 10:31). The second was dress reform (see 1 Cor. 6:19–20), and the third was Christian education (see Isa. 54:13). I had two young children at the time, ages seven and five, and I was fascinated with the thought of them being educated in a Christian school. I followed my convictions and enrolled them in Trinity Temple Academy in Hillside, New Jersey.

Several years later, I moved to Baltimore, Maryland, where my three younger sons were born. From grade one, they all attended a Christian school named Baltimore Junior Academy, with my youngest son experiencing Christian education all the way through college.

Even though it was expensive, and I could not afford it, I was sold out on the value of Christian education and soon realized that I could not afford *not* to send them. I had discovered that it really does pay much more than it costs. Consequently, I made up my mind that if I had to feast on oodles of noodles every night in order to educate my children, that's what I would do. And that's exactly what happened many an evening. I became an expert chef in different ways to fix this dish.

However, even with me sacrificing in the way I did, it was still a very difficult and challenging venture for me as a single parent. I remember one particular time when the school year was about to start, and I didn't even have their registration fees, not to mention tuition, so they were not allowed to attend class. I got down on my knees and prayed to God that He would make a way for us. One week passed by with no money. Two weeks passed by and still, no money. Out of concern, a well-meaning friend of mine suggested that I enroll them in public school just for that year, because I couldn't continue to keep them out of school.

I told them that public school was not an option for me because I knew my heavenly Father. What He has promised, He is also able to perform. My trust was in my God. He had brought me this far by faith, and like Jacob, while wrestling with the angel (see Gen. 32:26), I was determined not to let Him go until He blessed me.

> *When I opened the envelope, there was $800.00, the exact amount I needed to get them back in school!*

Well, three weeks went by, and my children were still not in school. I continued to pray, and then it happened!

One evening, I was sitting at my kitchen table talking with my friend who had advised me to consider public school, when someone knocked on my door. When I opened the door, it was the first elder from my church. He came in and presented me with an envelope and said that the Women's Ministries Department wanted to help a family at church and chose my children and me. When I opened the envelope, there was $800.00, the exact amount I needed to get them back in school! My friend sat there in disbelief and amazement at the Lord's miraculous intervention on my behalf. I thanked and praised God for taking care of us in such a wonderful way.

That day, the promise of Jeremiah 33:3 was fulfilled to me, "Call unto me, and I will answer thee, and show thee great and mighty things, which thou knowest not."

Praise be to God, from whom all blessings flow.

5

An "Oodles of Noodles" Blessing, Part 2

"If you believe, we believe."

As I sit here writing this experience, I can still hear the echo of those words ringing in my ears. It was the summer of 1988, and Irvin, my second oldest son, had just graduated from the eighth grade at Trinity Temple Academy in Hillside, New Jersey. I wanted him to continue his Christian education by attending Pine Forge Academy in Pine Forge, Pennsylvania, but I had no

27

money. I did the only thing that a child of God can do in a situation like this; I walked by faith.

I did not have a car at the time, so I prayed and asked God to please make a way. He impressed me to ask Daisy Rodgers (long-time literature evangelist) and her husband Uriah Rodgers (both of whom are now deceased) if they would take us there. They agreed, and so I packed my son's suitcase and school supplies, and off we went.

Even though Pine Forge was only a two-and-a-half-hour drive, it was one of the longest trips I've ever taken, partly because it was a journey of sheer faith and partly because Brother Rodgers didn't drive a mile above the speed limit! As I sat there in the back seat, praying, I looked over at my son, and our eyes met. He shook his head in disbelief as if to say, "My mother has lost her mind!" Then he said, "Mom, you're going to embarrass me."

I said, "Son, don't worry. God will come through for us." These words were spoken to encourage myself as well as him because I really didn't know quite what to expect upon arrival, but I knew that God was all that I possessed, and for me, that was enough.

When we finally arrived on the campus, there was orientation, forms to fill out, and long lines to stand in. We filled out all the necessary paperwork and received his class schedule. As we moved from line to line, my prayers were ascending to Jesus for divine intervention. The last line was the registrar. I was standing in line with literally not a penny in my pocket. I watched as parent after parent came and shelled out big bucks to register their children. All I had was a prayer and a promise, "But my God shall supply all your need according to His riches in glory by Christ Jesus" (Phil. 4:19). That was like money in the bank for me, so when it was my turn in line, I approached the registrar with confidence, believing that my Father's check would not bounce. When she asked me for the money, I told her that I didn't have any. She said that I would have to wait and talk to the principal.

By this time, my son was convinced that I was a few fries short of a Happy Meal, and I could see the stress and disappointment begin to form on his brow. As we sat there waiting to be called into the principal's office, I again reassured him that God would keep His promises. After about forty-five minutes, we were ushered in, and as we sat down, the principal said, "How can I help you?" Like Nehemiah, when he stood before King Artaxerxes, I darted a quick prayer up to heaven and said, "Lord, grant me favor in the sight of this man." I explained my dire situation to him, and my desire to give my son a Christian education at all cost. I shared with him what I would be able to contribute each month (which wasn't nearly enough to cover expenses) and told him that public school was not even a consideration for me. He leaned back in his chair and listened intently as I spoke.

When I finished, he leaned forward and looked at my son and me. That's when I heard some of the sweetest words to ever fall upon my ears. He said, "If you believe, we believe."

He told me that he was willing to work with me and gave my son clearance to attend class. He had prayer with us, and at that moment, all I could say was, "Wow, Lord. You did it!" My son was so overwhelmed that he began to cry, and tears filled my eyes, too, as I realized the magnitude of what God had done.

> *All I could say was, "Wow, Lord. You did it!"*

I thanked the principal for his kindness and understanding, and amidst tears of joy, we unpacked the car and got him settled in his dorm room. We embraced as I returned to the car minus one passenger. This time I didn't mind the slow ride back home. I felt as though we were riding on a cloud as I contemplated the goodness of God, and I was looking forward to getting home and enjoying ... you guessed it. A big bowl of oodles of noodles. M-mm ... delicious!

6

A "Cold Turkey" Miracle

I believe that the measure of true ministry is how much you are willing to sacrifice for the good of others. Jesus Christ is the very embodiment of selfless love and, as such, has set a perfect example for us to follow.

Sometimes, you have to get down into the trenches with people in order to help pull them out of the muck and mire of life's circumstances. That is exactly what happened to me in 1995. I was living and working in Baltimore, Maryland, at the time as a literature evangelist. While there, I met a young lady in her mid-twenties who had joined the church after attending evangelistic meetings conducted by Elder Henry J. Fordham III.

At first, she would sit in her window across the street from the tent and listen to the service. That gave the Holy Spirit opportunity to draw her. As she came closer, she began to yield, and when the meetings ended, she gave her heart to the Lord through baptism. She had two children whom she enrolled in Baltimore Jr. Academy, and that is how I first met this family. While living in Baltimore, I was the small literature coordinator. That entailed taking students out from Baltimore Jr. Academy to sell *Message Magazine*, which helped them to pay for their tuition.

The children's mother and I became good friends, and during the course of our friendship, I learned that she was struggling with a very serious drug addiction. She had been in and out of rehab centers for several years, would stay clean for a period of time, and then once again succumb to the stronghold that refused to loosen its grip on her.

Early one morning, around one o'clock, I was startled awake by the phone ringing. As I picked it up, I could hear her crying uncontrollably on the other end. Wiping the sleep from my eyes, I tried to make out as best I could what she was saying in between the sobs. "Jean, please help me. (sob) I can't (sob) do this anymore. (sob) I want to be delivered. (sob) Can you help (sob) me go "cold turkey?" I can't do it by myself. (sob) Will you help me, please?" (sob) The tone of her voice was one of desperation, and I knew that she had come to the end of her rope and was at a breaking point. I had no idea of what to do, but I prayed with her and gave the assurance of my support in any way possible.

As I drifted back off to sleep, I prayed that God would direct my steps, and indeed, He did. That morning, during my devotions, I talked to the Lord and said, "I don't know what to do." He said to me, "Are you willing?" I said, "Yes, Lord. I'm willing. Just show me what to do." He then directed me to a book called *Prescription for Nutritional Healing* by James and Phyllis Balch.

After praying and consulting the book, the Lord impressed me to purchase the following list of items from the health food store: (1) Vitamin B complex (reduces stress and helps to rebuild the liver), (2) calcium and magnesium (nourishes the central nervous system and helps control tremors by calming the body), (3) GABA (gamma-Aminobutyric acid) – (acts as a relaxant and lessens cravings), (4) L-tyrosine amino acid and valerian root combined every four hours (helps with withdrawals), (5) sodium ascorbate, buffered vitamin C (detoxifies the system and lessens the craving for the drug).

I picked up everything from the store, and we set the day and time that we would begin. I packed up a week's worth of clothes for myself and my three younger children who were at home, and when the day came, we headed over to her house. Upon arrival, I was not quite prepared for what I saw. She was lying on the sofa in the living room, unable to get up because she was too weak to walk or get in and out of bed. Her physical frame had deteriorated from around 130 pounds to less than ninety. I knelt by the side of the couch and held her hand as I prayed to God for mercy.

The next morning, we began our regimen. I took our children to school each morning, then came back and ministered to her until it was time to pick them up. Then I would fix dinner, make sure everyone's homework was done, and continue to take care of her through the night hours. The first three days were really rough. I had never witnessed anyone going through "cold turkey" withdrawal before, and it was a grueling experience.

Perspiration was pouring off of her like water, yet she felt as cold as ice inside. Then came the involuntary tremors, the cramps, and the vomiting, as her body began the process of detoxification. I patiently cleaned up after her and encouraged her that everything would be alright. I slept in the living room near her and would be awakened during the night to the sound of her crying out to God for help. I would get up and kneel by her side, praying to God for deliverance while wiping the sweat from her brow. This ordeal continued for three days, but on the fourth day, though still weak and unable to walk on her own, she could now sit up and eat a little soup. She was too weak to bathe, so I helped her in and out of the bathtub.

> *This ordeal continued for three days.*

By the fifth day, the vomiting had stopped, and she began to feel a little better. Praise God, by the seventh day, she had won the victory through Him who is more than conqueror! Amazing grace from an amazing God!! He delivered her from a drug addiction that had held her captive for more than fifteen years. What a wonderful Savior is Jesus, my Lord!

"Wherefore He is able to save them to the uttermost that come unto God by him, seeing he ever liveth to make intercession for them" (Heb. 7:25). Did we ever have a prayer and praise service that evening! I gathered the children together, and we all showered the Lord with praise and thanksgiving for His awesome deliverance and salvation.

After this experience, she looked like a brand-new person. In time, she regained all her weight and was even able to accompany me to Allegheny East Conference's camp meeting held that year (1995) at Hampton University in Hampton, Virginia.

Today, this beautiful child of God is drug-free and rejoicing in Jesus.

As I traveled back home with my children, I basked in the sunshine of God's love and thanked Him for giving me such a grand opportunity. To be a co-laborer with Christ in the salvation of souls is the greatest privilege that anyone can have, and I wondered to myself, "Where will the Lord lead you next, Jean?"

7

A Blessing Out of Tragedy

On October 30, 2000, Maryland State Trooper Edward M. Toatley was killed in the line of duty in Washington, DC. There was extensive media coverage and a nationwide manhunt for his killer. A few months later, in December, I received a lead card from a young lady who was interested in the *Bible Reference Library*, which is a twelve-volume Bible commentary and study combined. As I entered her home and we began to talk, she started to cry and told me that she was a friend of Officer Toatley, and was still grieving his death. She had many questions and needed some answers. Where was he? Was he in heaven? Was he in hell? She didn't know much about the Bible, and that's why she had sent in the card.

I was able to give her a brief study on the state of the dead and what happens when a person dies. I showed her how the *Bible Reference Library* would answer many of her questions and help her to understand the Bible better. She paid cash for the set that evening. I had prayer with her, and she was very grateful that I had come to her home.

I left her house with a sense of awe and wonder at the God of heaven and earth. He hears our faintest cry, and He always causes truth and the truth seeker to meet, even if it's at the intersection of a tragedy.

> *He always causes truth and the truth seeker to meet, even if it's at the intersection of a tragedy.*

God will not leave us in darkness when we're searching for light. His Word is indeed a lamp unto our feet and a light unto our path (see Psa. 119:105). Praise His holy name!

8
What If?

What if I hadn't knocked on her door that day? What if I had given in to my feelings and stayed home that particular day? It was a chilly morning in February of 2004 when I first met Felicia. I was dealing with my own issues and waging an uphill battle with depression. However, a fellow literature evangelist was waiting for me to pick her up so that we could go and knock on doors, so I pushed myself to get up.

We went to a high-rise building in Newark, New Jersey, that had twenty floors. We started at the top and worked our way down. When we got to the twelfth floor, I knocked on Felicia's door. She was very cordial and invited us in. She told us that she never opened her door for anyone because of the crime in the area, but as she looked through the peep-hole, the Lord said, "Open the door. These two ladies are different."

What if I hadn't knocked on her door that day?

As we sat at her kitchen table, it was evident that she was depressed. I asked her what was wrong. As she began to share her story, my own problems began to fade into the background as I listened attentively to her plight. She told us that in 2001, she had been diagnosed with colon cancer, and just that week, had been told that it had spread to her liver and lungs. In the midst of her pain, I sensed that she knew God, and she began to thank and praise Him for all that He had done for her. We had prayer with her and were able to leave two books in her home, *Peace Above the Storm* and *Christ's Object Lessons*.

When I returned home that evening, the Lord said to me, "There's something more that you can do for Felicia. I want you to show her how to juice fresh fruits and vegetables." I began to pray for wisdom and guidance and started doing some research concerning cancer. The next day, I went to the market and purchased various fruits and vegetables and took them to her house along with my juicer. She was overcome with gratitude that someone whom she had just met would do something of this magnitude for her. I would stop by every day and help her to juice.

In the coming months, Felicia's health began to improve. I drove her to Maryland to see a doctor that I knew, and what he said was amazing. He told her that on a scale of one to a thousand, the cancer was only 300. What was harming her more than the cancer was the heavy metal toxins from the chemotherapy she was taking. She was only supposed to be on it for six months, but she had been taking it for three years! What he told her next was really astounding. As he looked at the combination of fruits and vegetables that she was juicing, he said, "I can't tell you anymore to do other than what Ms. Good has shared with you. The only thing different that I would say is to increase the juicing to twice a day instead of once a day." I knew that God had spoken to me and had directed my steps. However, Felicia had been on chemotherapy for so long that she told me she was afraid to stop taking it. Felicia passed away in 2007.

During the three years that I knew her, we had become good friends. Thank God, I was able to give her Bible studies, and she attended church with me on several occasions. Felicia accepted Jesus as her personal Savior. She asked me a question one day after our Bible study that I will never forget. She said, "Miss Jean, if I decide not to get baptized in your church, are you going to stop being my friend?" I assured her that our friendship was secure regardless of her decision.

What if I see Felicia in heaven? Well, this is one "what if" that I don't have to wonder about because God says in

Romans 10:9, "If you confess with your mouth the Lord Jesus and believe in your heart that God raised Him from the dead, you will be saved" (NKJV). I'm going to be looking for Felicia on that day. What a day of rejoicing that will be!

I'm so glad that the Lord helped me to persevere that chilly day in 2004 and to hurdle past the "what ifs" in my own life. Felicia made such a significant impact on my life that I kept her picture on my dashboard for three years just as a reminder of the importance of my work as a literature evangelist.

9

A Gutter Blessing

The publishing ministry is a great work, second to none. It affords you an opportunity to sow beside all waters, reaching people from all ethnicities and walks of life. I am tremendously blessed to be a co-laborer with Christ through this amazing ministry.

One thing I have learned over the years is that, when you work for God, you never have to be concerned about the results of your labor. It may seem as though much of what you do is in vain, but you can be assured that the Lord of the harvest will water the seeds that you have sown, and in His timing, they will spring up and bear fruit. I am reminded of the following statement, "As canvassers or evangelists, you may not have had the success you prayed for, but remember that you do not know and cannot measure the result of faithful effort" (Colporteur Ministry, p. 114).

As literature evangelists, we put out lead cards in doctor's offices, community businesses, and from door to door, hoping to get a positive response from someone who is interested in knowing more about the Lord. But occasionally, the lead cards can wind up in some out of the way places. One day, I had an experience that illustrates this point.

I received a card from a lady who was interested in obtaining a set of *The Bible Story* for children by Arthur S. Maxwell. The card was dirty, tattered, and torn, and the person's name and address were barely legible. It's a wonder that it even made it through the mail in that condition.

When I went to visit her, I was curious to know where she had gotten the card. This is her miraculous story. She told me that she grew up attending Trinity Temple Seventh-day Adventist Church in Newark, New Jersey, and that her grandparents had been very influential in her upbringing. When she was a little girl, her grandmother would read to her from *The Bible Story*, and she never forgot it. As she grew up, several things happened in her life to discourage her, and she wound up leaving the church around the age of eighteen or nineteen.

"God, where can I find those books?"

Now that she was in her forties and had grandchildren of her own, she wanted them to have *The Bible Story* books that had blessed her as a child, but she hadn't seen them in years and didn't know where to find them. She prayed and said, "God, where can I find those books?"

Three days later, she was getting out of a taxi and stepped into some mud. As she looked down, she couldn't believe her eyes. There was a brochure advertising *The Bible Story*, lying in the gutter! Even though it was torn and dirty, she picked it up and filled it out as best she could, hoping and praying that she would get back a response.

She was so happy that I came to her home and was elated as she purchased the books for her grandchildren. She also told me that she was considering coming back to church. What a wonderful testimony to the power of a prayer-hearing, prayer-answering God! There is a statement in *Colporteur Ministry* that fits this experience to a T: "We should treat as a sacred treasure every line of printed matter containing present truth. Even the fragments of a pamphlet or of a periodical should be regarded as of value. Who can estimate the influence that a torn page containing the truths of the third angel's message may have upon the heart of some seeker after truth?" (p. 151).

That lead card had originally been placed in a doctor's office. Someone took it, decided that they weren't really interested in it, and threw it away, but God watched over that brochure because He knew that one of His children was praying for light. He knew that on a certain day, at a particular time, His daughter would be stepping out of a taxi and into a gutter filled with blessings. "Ask, and it shall be given you; seek, and ye shall find; knock, and it shall be opened unto you" (Matt. 7:7).

10

Blessings from a Curve Ball

All parents desire their children to grow up and live wholesome, productive lives. Unfortunately, these dreams don't always come to fruition. Sometimes, life throws a curveball our way, an unexpected pitch that we're not quite prepared for. It hits us below the belt and knocks us to the ground, and we find ourselves struggling to get back up again.

I have sustained several curveballs as a parent, but with each unexpected blow, God has picked me up, dusted me off, and pointed my feet back in the direction of home plate. Such has been the case with my fourth son, Isaiah. In August of 2005, at the age of twenty, he left my home for good to begin a journey of his own, a journey of homelessness that, at the time of this writing, has lasted for thirteen years.

I still vividly remember the night that he left. I knew that I had reached my limit of endurance because my stress level was so high that I could only function a maximum of two hours at a time. Then, I would have to lie down for an extended period of time just to regroup and re-energize myself. The pressure was so great that my immune system began to break down, and every three weeks, I was sick with the flu. The Lord knew that the issues I was dealing with concerning Isaiah had exceeded my power to cope. He said to me that August evening, "Let him go, and let Me have him."

I recall the moment that I heard the sound of the door close and realized that he had stepped out into the night, not knowing where it would take him. I lay on my bed and wept, pouring out my soul to my heavenly Father. I said, "Lord, where is he going to go? How is he going to make it?" I asked God to please take care of him and to comfort me through His Word.

The Lord knows just what each one of His children stands in need of, and He relates to us accordingly. Whenever I ask God to speak to me through His Word, this is how He responds to me. After praying for the guidance of the Holy Spirit, I open my Bible, and wherever it lands, God speaks directly to me about my situation or about whatever He wants me to know for that day. This is the way He has communicated with me for over thirty years!

I love the Lord because He is such a personal God. He will indeed meet you at the very point of your need. Jesus has many names, but my favorite is Emmanuel (God with us). God's presence in my life means more to me than anything in this world. Just to know that He is with me gives me an assurance and security that I cannot find anywhere else.

So, I opened my Bible, and God spoke to me through 1 Corinthians 15:58: "Therefore, my beloved brethren, be ye steadfast, unmovable, always abounding in the work of the Lord, forasmuch as ye know that your labor is not in vain in the Lord." As I ran a cross-reference on the text, it took me to 2 Chronicles 15:7, "Be ye strong therefore, and let not your hands be weak: for your work shall be rewarded."

He then spoke to my spirit and said, "You have been a good mother. You have planted the seed of My Word in the hearts of your children. I will see to it that it is watered and bears fruit. You have done all that you can do, so let him go and let Me have him."

I have held onto these promises for the past thirteen years because knowing that my son is living homeless on the streets has been a very hard pill for me to swallow as a mother. No matter what your child has said or done, no matter how many times they have hurt you and caused you pain, you never stop loving your child because your love for them supersedes any amount of heartache that you may have endured. But every time this horse pill gets stuck in my throat, the Lord always comforts me and gives me hope. Here are two of many such instances.

I remember when Hurricane Irene hit in 2011, everyone was warned to stay off the streets and seek shelter. I was sitting by the window in my living room, worried about Isaiah.

> *Lord, please have mercy on my son and protect him. Please let me know that he's okay.*

"Where is he, Lord? Where is he going to go in this storm? Lord, please have mercy on my son and protect him. Please let me know that he's okay."

Ten minutes after I finished praying, the phone rang. It was my youngest son Simeon. He said, "Mom, have you heard from Isaiah?" I said, "No, but I just finished praying about it." He said that Isaiah had contacted him on Facebook and told him to let me know that he was okay. Ah! "And it shall come to pass, that before they call, I will answer; and while they are yet speaking, I will hear" (Isa. 65:24).

The very next day, Isaiah called me with an amazing testimony! He said he had been walking down the street, with no place to go. The hurricane was about to make landfall, and he didn't know what to do. He said he prayed and asked God to help him, and as he finished praying, a friend of his, whom he hadn't seen in a couple of years, was walking toward him. His friend asked him where he was going in this storm, and when Isaiah told him he didn't know, the friend invited him to come home with him until the storm was over.

"Bless the Lord, O my soul: and all that is within me, bless His holy name!" (Ps. 103:1) What a mighty God we serve! He truly does hear the faintest cry from the weakest of His children. I was overjoyed at what my Lord had done, and was able to digest this bitter pill a little better, knowing that He had heard my cry.

There was another instance where I had not seen or heard from Isaiah in months. I discovered that he was incarcerated and was due in court on a particular day. I decided to go, but also had to travel to Pine Forge, Pennsylvania, on the same day. The court hearing was at noon in Newark, New Jersey. To travel from my home to Pine Forge, and then to Newark, would be a 200-mile trip. I left early that morning, praying that I would be able to get back in time. There was traffic along the way coming back, and by the time I got to Newark and found a parking space, it was 12:10.

When I arrived at the courthouse, there was a line for security. When I finally got through security, I went to the wrong courtroom and had to locate the correct one. My heart was pounding with anxiety and stress from rushing all around and not wanting to be late. As soon as I opened the right courtroom door, this is what I heard, "Is anyone here for Isaiah Good?" Unbelievable! Gasping for breath, I raised my hand and said, "I am!"

What an absolutely amazing God we serve. Psalm 32:8 says it best, "I will instruct thee and teach thee in the way which thou shalt go: I will guide thee with mine eye." He had taken me 200 miles through traffic and delays, and caused me to enter that courtroom at the exact time that the judge was calling Isaiah's name! I went home consoled and encouraged by the mercy and lovingkindness of my Father. He reminded me that day that Isaiah is indeed in the palm of His hands, and that He is ever mindful of my pain. I am learning that God's timing in my life is always perfect, and knows no haste or delay. Praise His holy name!

11

A Surprise Blessing

The year was 2007. It was a hot summer day in Trenton, New Jersey. Robert Moses and I were on opposite sides of the street, knocking on doors in preparation for an evangelistic meeting at the Mt. Sinai SDA Church under the leadership of Pastor Paul Turner.

As I passed by, there was a lady standing on the sidewalk in front of a senior citizen complex, so I stopped and asked her if she wouldn't mind taking a brief community survey. She said sure and indicated that she would be interested in Bible studies as well. We had prayer and set up a time to begin her first study. This was my first meeting with Joan Picott.

A few days later, as we were working in that same neighborhood, it began to rain. I suggested to Brother Moses that we go into the senior building, but you needed to know someone in order to gain entry. I rang Joan Picott's bell, and she buzzed us in. We were able to visit all the apartments and picked up three additional Bible study interests. I began studying with Joan, and when the evangelistic meetings started, she, along with many of the residents, attended nightly. At the end of the series, several of the tenants took their stand and were baptized, but Joan was not one of them. We lost touch, and I wondered whatever became of her.

Two years later, I received a call from Pastor Turner one evening. He said, "Sister Good, I have a newly baptized member at my church who loves to give out tracts and is interested in becoming a literature evangelist." He gave me her first name and asked me to contact her.

I called, and as we began to talk, I remarked to myself that her voice sounded vaguely familiar. Little did I know that she was thinking the same thing about me. After a while, she said, "Wait a minute! Is this the same Jean that prayed for me outside of my building and gave me Bible studies?" I said, "Yes," and discovered that I was talking to Joan Picott! She said that she had often thought about me and wondered where I was. She didn't come in through that first baptism, but continued to attend Mt. Sinai and eventually got baptized several months later.

I had the privilege of training her to become a literature evangelist and working with her for over a year before she passed away in 2012. What a wonderful Savior is Jesus, my Lord! I have learned from doing ministry that you never have to worry about the results of your work. It may sometimes seem as though your labor has gone by the wayside, but God assures us in His word that "As the

> *I have learned from doing ministry that you never have to worry about the results of your work.*

rain comes down, and the snow from heaven, and do not return there, but water the earth, and make it bring forth and bud, that it may give seed to the sower and bread to the eater, so shall My word be that goes forth out of My mouth; It shall not return unto me void, but it shall accomplish that which I please, and it shall prosper in the thing for which I have sent it" (Isa. 55:10–11, NKJV).

I'm looking forward to seeing Joan Picott again, but this time, it won't be on the sidewalk in front of a senior citizen's building in Trenton, New Jersey. It will be on the streets of gold in front of her mansion in the New Jerusalem. Hallelujah! Or maybe we'll meet in front of mine. Who knows?

12

The Blessing of *Blessings*

S ome time ago, I was at a publishing leadership meeting in Charleston, South Carolina. There were marketing representatives there from both the Review and Herald and Pacific Press Publishing Associations. They were showing us some new materials that were hot off the press. One of them was a book entitled *Blessings* by Jerry D. Thomas, which is a modern adaptation of E.G. White's book, *Thoughts from The Mount of Blessing*.

As we previewed the book, most of the publishing leaders (myself included) were not happy with the picture of Jesus that was portrayed on the front cover. We felt that since we were working in urban areas, the illustration should be more representative of our clientele. Each publishing leader was given a copy of the book. I took mine to my room.

The next day, after the meeting was over, I went back to my room and met a lady from housekeeping at my door. As I approached her, I heard the Holy Spirit speak very clearly and distinctly in my mind, "Give her the book." I greeted her and said, "I have something for you." I went into my room, got the book, and when I handed it to her, her mouth dropped open, and tears filled her eyes. She looked at me and said, "You're giving me this book?" I said, "Yes." She said, "How did you know that I wanted this book?" Well, her response puzzled me because the book had just come off the press and was not yet available for purchase, so I said, "You wanted this book?"

"Yes," she said. "Last night I saw the cover of this book in the trash can. It caught my attention, so I took it out and read it. I said, 'Lord, how can I get a copy of this book?' And here you are the next day giving it to me."

Needless to say, I was flabbergasted! I couldn't believe what I was hearing. The only ones who had access to the book were the publishing leaders, so I knew that it had to be one of us who had thrown the cover in the trash. She thanked me profusely for her new-found treasure and hugged *Blessings* to her chest with both hands. I asked for her number and kept in touch with her for a while. She told me that she was taking her time reading the book so that she could digest it because there were wonderful things in it that she had never heard before.

Then she said something that I will never forget: "I have to be honest with you, Jean. When you first told me that you had something for me, I thought it was money, but little did I know that what you've given me is more important than any amount of money that I could have received."

My heart was humbled, and this experience taught me a valuable lesson. While we were haggling over the color of the picture, God was preparing someone's heart to receive the contents of the book. God is an awesome Savior, and when it comes to spiritual things, I will never again "judge a book by its cover."

13

A Thanksgiving to Remember

I never know where He will lead me next because the Lord always takes me on an adventure when I work for Him. It was 2012, and my now-deceased colleague Robert Moses and I were working in a joint evangelistic meeting between the Church of the Oranges, under the leadership of Pastor D. Robert Kennedy, and the Berean SDA Church in Newark, under the leadership of Pastor Ivor Keizer.

The Church of the Oranges hosted a huge job fair one Sunday that drew over 2,000 people from various areas! We distributed more than 1,000 copies of *The Great Hope* and *Steps to Christ* and were given a list of about 250 names from the community to follow up on. As Brother Moses and I were contacting people and making visitations, we met a young lady who had attended the job fair. She was desperately looking for work and was very happy that we had come to encourage and pray with her. She shared an apartment with her sister and her three children, along with two nieces. This family had experienced a lot of tragedy in their lives, and over the next few years, I began to minister to them, and today, these two sisters are like daughters to me.

I remember one Thanksgiving Eve that the Lord impressed me to go shopping for them.

I remember one Thanksgiving Eve that the Lord impressed me to go shopping for them. It was the most memorable Thanksgiving of my life. They gave me a list of all the things they wanted, which I happily purchased and delivered.

Then something happened that touched my heart at the very core of my being. As I was waiting for the elevator, this young lady came out of her apartment with all five of her nieces and nephews. They ranged in age from three to fifteen and were all standing in a line from the youngest to the eldest. Each one came up to me and hugged me as they said thank you.

I stepped into the elevator with tears streaming down my face, hoping that no one else would get on. As I walked to my car, I thanked and praised the Lord for once again answering my prayer. Every day that He gives me breath, I ask Him to let me be a rainbow in someone else's cloud, and He always causes someone to cross my path to whom I can minister. To God be the glory!

> *One day, I may die without saying goodbye to you, but I will never forget to say thank you.*

Several months later, I woke up early one morning to the sound of my computer. I had an old desktop and must have had the volume up too high because the sound awakened me, letting me know that I had an email. It was a beautiful quotation from this young lady, and this is what it said exactly:

"One day, I may die without saying goodbye to you, but I will never forget to say thank you because you hold the most loveliest part in my life."

These are the things that mean the most to me. The treasures of this world are of little value, but to know that, by God's grace, you have helped to lighten someone else's burdens is of endless worth. I like what my heavenly Father says:

"If you extend your soul to the hungry And satisfy the afflicted soul, Then your light shall dawn in the darkness,

And your darkness shall be as the noonday. The Lord will guide you continually, And satisfy your soul in drought, And strengthen your bones; You shall be like a watered garden, And like a spring of water, whose waters do not fail" (Isa. 58:10–11, NKJV).

May it be even so in my life, Lord Jesus. Amen.

14

The Blessings of a Dog Bite

The literature evangelism work is a great work and one that has been ordained by God Himself as a means of leading people back to the study of His Word. I am privileged to be a part of this mighty work and to see God's care and providential workings in my life. I am reminded of the Scripture in Isaiah 54:17 that says, "No weapon that is formed against thee shall prosper."

My car gave out on me in August of 2013. I had no transportation, so I decided to just knock on doors in my neighborhood. While out working one day in September, I was bitten in the stomach by a dog. When I first approached the house, there was no dog to be seen or heard. The door was cracked, but the screen door was closed. I put my bag down, and when I reached up to ring the bell, a huge German Shepherd came barreling through the screen door and bit me in the stomach. I barely had time to react, as I tumbled backward down the stairs and into the bushes.

He attacked me again, but this time grabbed hold of my skirt and tore it to shreds. The owner ran out and was able to subdue him. She told me that he had never ever done that to anyone before, not even the mailman. I knew that it was an attack from the enemy.

This may seem like a strange reaction, but I remember saying to myself, "Now, Lord, I

I've got to leave some books in this home!

know that You didn't send me to this house just to get bitten by a dog. I've got to leave some books in this home!

The owner brought me into the house, where I was able to clean myself up a bit. I was still able to canvass her, torn skirt and all, and by God's grace, left three books in her home—*God's Answers to Your Questions*, *Foods That Heal*, and *Cat In The Cage* (a children's book).

She gave me a ride home, and despite the incident, we became friends. I spent the next three months recuperating from this injury, but I know that God's Word will not return unto Him void. I didn't expect to get bitten by a dog that day, but I do expect to reap a harvest of souls from it. Thank You, Jesus.

15

The Trash Can Check

Being a literature evangelist without a car is no easy task, especially in the wintertime, when you live in a town that has no public transportation, and you have places to go, people to see, and books to deliver.

In 2013–14, I was without a car for nine months, but if you know anything about our heavenly Father, you know that He is a way-maker. He always provides a "ram in the thicket," as it were, and never leaves His children without a testimony to glorify His name.

Since I was not able to go to the people, God sent the people to me. I began to receive numerous phone calls from those who wanted to purchase books, and in the nine months that I was without transportation, the Lord blessed me to be able to deliver over $15,000 worth of Bible-based literature. Praise

> *If you know anything about our heavenly Father, you know that He is a way-maker.*

His holy name! He sent help my way from various sources, using neighbors, friends, and church members to assist me. One sister in Christ, who had only known me for a short while, gave me her car to use for three weeks so that I could do my work. Now, who does that?! It was nothing but the blessings of the Lord.

One day I was sitting in my living room, looking out the window. I had begun to get a little weary of this trial that had lasted three months shy of a year and was talking to the Lord about it. There are many things that I love about the Lord, one of which is the fact that I can come to Him and express exactly how I'm feeling at the moment, whether up or down, with no pretense. I don't have to be phony with my God.

As soon as I finished pouring out my heart to my Father, the phone rang, and it was my youngest son, Simeon. He asked me if I had received some mail that he was expecting. I told him the only thing that had come was some advertisement (or so I thought) from some college, which I assumed was junk mail because he had already graduated, and so I had thrown it into my bathroom trash can without even opening it. I had passed by the trash for several days, with the thought in mind of emptying it, but was a bit depressed about my circumstances and just didn't feel like going downstairs to the dumpster.

I sensed an urgency in my son's reply: "Mom, *please* tell me that you didn't throw it away! It's really important." I told him to hold on as I rummaged through the trash can, trying to retrieve the envelope. I finally found it, and when I came back to the phone, he exhaled with a big sigh of relief and said, "Thank God! Mom, you scared me for a moment." He asked me to open the letter, and when I did, I gasped in unbelief and shock. There inside that envelope was a check for $5,000! I didn't know that he had been taking some courses at another college and had received a refund from a Parent Plus loan that I had taken out for him a few years earlier. He said, "Mom, I wanted to surprise you with money to buy a car."

I couldn't believe it! In a matter of moments, my sadness was turned into joy, my trials to triumph, as I realized what my Savior had done for me. I thanked my son immensely for his thoughtfulness in looking out for his mother. I was so overwhelmed that I fell on my knees in gratitude and thanksgiving to God for His lovingkindness and His tender mercies towards me.

As I think about this amazing experience, I realize that we've all done it before—thrown things in the garbage by mistake, or in my case intentionally, not knowing that it is something of value, and I wonder to myself, "How often do we treat God's word in like manner?" We may not literally toss it into the trash, but sometimes by our actions, we show how lightly we esteem its worth and do not discern its true import.

Many times, we neglect to study the Bible on a daily basis, and when we do, it is merely a surface reading, not really taking the time to dig deeper into the gold mine of His Word. Matthew 13:44 declares that "The kingdom of heaven is like unto treasure hid in a field; the which when a man hath found, he hideth, and for joy goeth and selleth all that he hath, and buyeth that field."

God's precious promises to us are scattered all throughout the Bible, like hidden nuggets of treasure. However, we must search diligently to find them and appropriate each one to our particular situation. If I had known that $5,000 check was in the trash, I would have done whatever it took to find it, even if it meant getting my hands dirty!

Proverbs 16:9 says, "A man's heart deviseth his way; but the Lord directeth his steps." I intended to empty that trash. For five days, I passed by and lamented because it was still there, but the Spirit of the Lord constrained me and used my lethargy and procrastination to bring a blessing to me and glory to His name. When we are at our wit's end and don't know what to do, we can be sure that God is setting us up for a new beginning. "Wait on the Lord: be of good courage, and He shall strengthen thine heart: wait, I say, on the Lord" (Ps. 27:14).

He may not come exactly when you want Him to, but He's always on time. Hallelujah!

16
A Sunday Go-to-Meeting Blessing

During the time that I was without a car for nine months, I accumulated several lead cards from potential customers who were interested in purchasing literature. After the Lord blessed me with transportation, I began to contact them. As I started flipping through the cards, I noticed that one of them was from a pastor of another Christian church in Newark, whom I had previously visited some time ago, but was not able to canvass at the time.

Unfortunately, three years had gone by, and I wondered if he still remembered me. I dialed his number, and after re-introducing myself, to my surprise, he did remember and confirmed that he was still interested. He invited me to come to his church the following Sunday to make a presentation before his congregation. I arrived at 11:00 AM and joined them for the worship service.

Afterward, I was able to present an array of health and character-building materials. Ten of his members signed up to receive home visitations. I thanked the pastor for such an awesome opportunity and presented him with a deluxe copy of *The Great Controversy*, a powerful book on church history, Bible prophecy, and end-time events, by E. G. White.

During my visit to one member in her home, she said, "It was such a blessing when you came to our church that Sunday. I've been praying to God to help me to understand the Bible, and then you showed up with all of these wonderful books." She purchased the *Heritage Bible*, and *Foods and Their Healing Power*, and told me that she especially wanted the book I had given to her pastor, *The Great Controversy*. We have now become friends, and she has expressed an interest in

> *By God's grace, in one hour I was able to distribute 400 copies of* **The Great Hope.**

attending the Allegheny East Conference's annual ten-day camp meeting in Pine Forge, Pennsylvania.

While visiting another member, he told me about a unity day rally being hosted in Newark by various community churches and organizations. By God's grace, in one hour I was able to distribute 400 copies of *The Great Hope*, an abbreviated copy of *The Great Controversy*.

Who knows where all of this will lead? God says in Isaiah 55:11 that His word will not return unto Him void, "but it shall accomplish that which I please, and it shall prosper in the thing whereto I sent it." I'm sure that, when I get to heaven, I'll realize the full impact of that Sunday Go-To- Meeting Blessing. What a mighty God we serve.

17

The Bible Reference
Library Goes to College

In October of 2014, I was at a monthly ministerium
meeting with the area pastors of northern New Jersey.
Also present at the meeting were several representatives from Pillar College, a Christian institution located in
downtown Newark. As I sat there listening to the presentation being made, the Holy Spirit whispered in my ear,
"Why don't you see if you can place the *Bible Reference*

Library into Pillar College?" The *Bible Reference Library* is a twelve-volume commentary and Bible study on the Old and New Testaments.

I tossed the idea around in my head for a while, and about a month later, I called Pillar College and was given the number of the appropriate person to contact but received no response after several attempts. I began to pray and ask the Lord for further directions. He told me to contact Dr. Ralph Grant, who was present at the ministerium meeting and is the Director of Operations and Public Relations at Pillar College. Dr. Grant is a Seventh-day Adventist Christian who is living out his faith in the workplace. Everyone who enters his office receives a copy of the book *The Desire of Ages*, by E.G. White, which is one of the volumes in the *Bible Reference Library* series! When I shared with him what the Lord had placed on my heart, he was elated and said that he would set up an appointment for me with two of his colleagues that he had in mind.

When I arrived at Dr. Grant's office, I was able to meet and make a presentation to the librarian and to the Director of the Bi-lingual Entry Degree (B.L.E.N.D) program, Dr. John Muñiz. The B.L.E.N.D. program is designed to assist Spanish-speaking students. During the course of the presentation, I learned that, in addition to being a professor at Pillar College, Dr. Muñiz was also the pastor of the Second Reformed Church in Jersey City, New Jersey. He was very impressed with the literature and decided to purchase the entire twelve-volume series for his church library.

What an awesome God we serve! It took several months to finalize the transaction, but praise God, I was able to deliver the goods to him in May of 2015. Who knows what will be the final outcome of this? Only eternity can tell, and I plan to be there to see it all unfold.

18
How God Carried Carrian

Ilove the message found in Isaiah 46:3–4: "Hearken unto me, O house of Jacob, and all the remnant of Israel, which are borne by me from the belly, which are carried from the womb: And even to your old age I am he; and even to hoar hairs will I carry you: I have made, and I will bear; even I will carry, and will deliver you." I am drawn to this passage because it gives such comfort and reassurance by reminding me that no matter what happens in my life experience, I am kept safe in the arms of my heavenly Father from the cradle to the grave.

I had the privilege of seeing this promise fulfilled in the life of a remarkable woman by the name of Carrian. I first met Carrian in the spring of 2015, while working in an evangelistic effort with the Bethel Seventh-day Adventist Church in Jersey City, New Jersey, under the leadership of Pastor Troy Levy.

From our very first encounter, I perceived that God's hand was upon her and that she was a very special lady.

> *From our very first encounter, I perceived that God's hand was upon her and that she was a very special lady.*

I was following up on a list of people in the community who had previously taken the Amazing Facts Bible course. This was definitely a divine appointment because I started out intending to visit her first, as she was the nearest on my list. However, the Holy Spirit impressed me to save her for last. I have found that when you are doing God's work, He will lead you and guide you, directing your every step.

When I arrived at her home, she was just exiting her gate. The bells at her apartment building were not working, and there were no names on display, so I wouldn't have been able to get in if I had come earlier. What a God!

I shared with her the reason for my visit and offered her a copy of *Steps to Christ*. She was overjoyed to receive the book and told me that my coming was a direct answer from God. She said that she had just finished crying out to

God for a breakthrough in her life and was on the verge of giving up. I listened in awestruck wonder at the mercy and goodness of God, as Carrian told her story.

She had been stabbed seventeen times with all her major organs punctured and was left on the street for dead! As a result of this traumatic attack, she had suffered multiple strokes and heart attacks and had also developed cancer. Yet through it all, the Lord had graciously spared her life and was still carrying her, for which she was very grateful.

We seemed to bond instantly, as we talked together about the goodness of the Lord. This was not even a *third* of what she had endured in her life. She was still facing some very daunting health challenges, but this woman's faith in God was so evident and so strong, I have often compared it with that of Abraham! Carrian came to church with me during the evangelistic meetings, and we have become great friends. She is such an encouragement to me in my life and ministry.

In June of 2017, the enemy once again tried to take her life. I was sitting in the prayer garden at the annual ten-day camp meeting in Pine Forge, Pennsylvania, when I received a frantic call from Carrian. She asked me to pray because two men had just entered her home and threatened her at gunpoint. A family member owed them a large sum of money and was nowhere to be found. They told her that if she didn't come up with the money within five days, they were going to kill her!

I immediately went into prayer mode and entreated the Lord on her behalf. I assured her that the captain of

the Lord's host would fight this battle for her. I directed
her attention to several Scripture promises: "No weapon
that is formed against thee shall prosper; and every tongue
that shall rise against thee in judgment thou shalt con-
demn" (Isa. 54:17); "When the enemy shall come in like a
flood, the spirit of the Lord shall lift up a standard against
him" (Isa. 59:19), and, "The angel of the Lord encampeth round about them that fear him, and delivereth them"
(Ps. 34:7).

After I hung up the phone, I sat there for a while and
began to plead with my heavenly Father. "Father, I know
you've got this. Father, please intervene and fight this battle for Carrian. She's been through so much pain and suffering in her life. Please deliver her."

At that moment, the Holy Spirit brought a Scripture
to mind. "Verily I say unto you, Whatsoever ye shall bind
on earth shall be bound in heaven: and whatsoever ye shall
loose on earth shall be loosed in heaven. Again I say unto
you, that if two of you shall agree on earth as touching
any thing that they shall ask, it shall be done for them of
my Father which is in heaven. For where two or three are
gathered together in my name, there I am in the midst of
them" (Matt. 18:18–20).

I looked around the prayer garden and said, "Lord,
I need someone to pray with me concerning this." I saw
Pastor Carlos McConico of the Ebenezer Seventh-day
Adventist Church in Philadelphia enter the prayer gar-
den. I got up and approached him. I told him that I had a
dire emergency and needed special prayer, but I had to be

certain that he understood the urgency of my request, for this was no ordinary prayer that was needed. No, not the kind of prayer that simply says, "Lord, please help Carrian, Amen." I'm talking about the kind of prayer that gets in God's face, stays in God's face, and wrestles with Him like Jacob until the victory is won. I just felt as though Jesus was in control of the situation and would surely deliver her, and I was determined not to let Him go until He did just that!

> *I needed someone to pray with me who knew what it meant to engage in spiritual warfare.*

I needed someone to pray with me who knew what it meant to engage in spiritual warfare, and so, like Jesus when questioning Peter by the seashore, I looked him in the eye and said, "Pastor McConico, do you know the power of prayer?" He said, "Yes." I asked him a second time, "Do you really know the power of prayer?" He said, "Yes, I know the power of prayer." I then asked him a third time, "Do you *really* know the power of prayer and what it can do?" He looked at me sincerely and said, "Yes, Sis. I know what prayer can do."

At that, I was satisfied that I had the right person and began to tell him about Carrian's dilemma. We sat together in the prayer garden and had fervent intercession on her behalf. I thanked him, and he assured me that he would continue to pray about her situation. I also called Charmaine Simms, my friend and colleague in ministry from the First Seventh-day Adventist Church of Paterson, New Jersey, who is a known prayer warrior.

Even though I had duties to perform at camp meeting, I prayed without ceasing for the God of heaven to intervene, and every spare moment that I got, I either went to the prayer garden or knelt by the bed in my hotel room, pouring out my petitions to my Father. I called Carrian each morning as we counted down the days.

We prayed together, and I encouraged her to hold on to God's promises with the assurance that the Lord would honor His word the same way He did for Hezekiah, king of Judah, when Sennacherib, king of Assyria came against him. The Lord sent this message of hope and encouragement to Hezekiah through the prophet Isaiah,

> *"Carrian, don't worry. These men will not even step foot in your house again!"*

"Therefore thus saith the Lord concerning the king of Assyria, He shall not come into this city, nor shoot an arrow there, nor come before it with shields, nor cast a bank against it. By the way that he came, by the same shall he return, and shall not come into this city, saith the Lord. For I will defend this city to save it for mine own sake, and for my servant David's sake" (Isa. 37:33–35).

That very night, deliverance was given, for the angel of the Lord destroyed 185,000 soldiers of the Assyrian army! My spirit was so confident that God would protect her, that I said with holy boldness and a faith that would not be denied, "Carrian, don't worry. These men will not even step foot in your house again!"

The evening before they were to return, we prayed together, and I told her to call me the next day with her praise report. I spent the better part of the night in prayer and supplication to my God. The following day, as I sat under the pavilion for Sabbath services, my prayers were still ascending heavenward, as I awaited her much-anticipated call.

Noon, no call. At 2:00 p.m., Sabbath service was over, and still, no call. I went back to my hotel room, got down on my knees, and cried out to God for about an hour. When I finished praying, I sat on the side of the bed, and at 4:00 p.m. on July 1, 2017, my cell phone rang. Praise God, it was Carrian!

I listened with bated breath as she gave me a detailed account of what happened. She had spent the day in prayer and fasting, and they *never* returned to her home. She learned that they had gone to someone else's house and confessed, saying that they had mysteriously had a change of heart and didn't want to hurt anyone!!

Can you believe it?!!! Oh, glory to God in the highest. He had done just what He said He would do. He changed the purpose and intent of their evil plans and redirected their steps. Oh, magnify the Lord with me and let us exalt His name together. What a mighty God we serve! He is "able to do exceeding abundantly above all that we ask or think, according to the power that worketh in us" (Eph. 3:20). Oh, praise His holy name!!

Reader, I can't even begin to express to you how I felt at that moment. I was so overcome with emotion that I fell down before the awesome majesty and power of a covenant-keeping God and wept like a baby, thanking and praising Him for His miraculous intervention in answer to prayer. Carrian and I were both very grateful for the fulfillment of Psalm 91 that day:

> He that dwelleth in the secret place of the most High shall abide under the shadow of the Almighty. I will say of the Lord, He is my refuge and my fortress: my God; in Him will I trust. Surely he shall deliver thee from the snare of the fowler, and from the noisome pestilence. He shall cover thee with His feathers, and under His wings shalt thou trust: His truth shall be thy shield and buckler. Thou shalt not be afraid for the terror by night; nor for the arrow that flieth by day; Nor for the pestilence that walketh in darkness; nor for the destruction that wasteth at noonday.... Because thou hast made the Lord, which is my refuge, even the most High, thy habitation; There shall no evil befall thee, neither shall any plague come nigh thy dwelling. For He shall give His angels charge over thee, to keep thee in all thy ways (verses 1–11).

I believe with all my heart that prayer and faith are the most powerful weapons on earth. We were already close, but since this experience, Carrian and I have grown even closer as sisters in Christ. One day we were talking, and she said to me, "I want you to teach me all about the Sabbath. Whatever God has for me to do, that's what I want to do." So now, every Friday evening, we open up the Sabbath together with worship over the phone.

She is still confronted with many life-threatening health issues, and the doctors have told her that 2018 would be her last Christmas, but that's not her major concern. The only thing she wants to know is, in her own words, "What does my Daddy say? He has the last word." And indeed He does, "For assuredly, I say to you, if you have faith as a mustard seed, you will say to this mountain, 'Move from here to there,' and it will move; and nothing will be impossible for you" (Matt. 17:20, NKJV).

Oh, "Thanks be to God for His unspeakable gift" (2 Cor. 9:15).

19

The Twenty-Nine
Year Blessing

In May of 2016, I received some disturbing news concerning my financial future, but the Lord prepared me for it by performing a miracle for me five days before I received the news.

In 1987, my second son, Irvin, was an eighth-grader at Trinity Temple Academy in Hillside, New Jersey. At that time, a church member came to me and said that she would like to assist me with his school fees. However, due to unforeseen circumstances, it never materialized.

That eighth-grader is now forty-two years old at the time of this writing. This same church member came to me in May of 2016, twenty-nine years later, and said, "I promised you a long time ago that I would help you with your son's tuition, and I want to

> *The Lord's timing is always perfect.*

keep that promise to you." She gave me a beautiful card and $500.00. The message found in the card was profound. It read: "God is good, God is faithful, God is changeless. So what is there for you to worry about?"

When I received the disturbing news five days later, the Lord said to me, "If I can keep a promise that was made to you twenty-nine years ago, surely I can take care of any other situation in your life." The Lord's timing is always perfect. This experience has taught me that God's plans for my life are always on schedule. "Commit thy way unto the Lord; trust also in him; and he shall bring it to pass" (Ps. 37:5).

20

The Bedbugs Didn't Bite

On March 15, 2016, I went to work intent on distributing *The Great Hope* in the business community of Montclair, New Jersey. I had a specific location in mind, but as I was driving along, the Holy Spirit impressed me to stop at a different area in Montclair and distribute them there.

I got out of my car and proceeded to go in and out of the business establishments. I entered a Chinese restaurant and handed the lady behind the counter a copy, which she gladly received. A lady was waiting for her order, and I handed her a book as well. As we both walked outside, we began to talk about the goodness of the Lord. She asked me what church I attended, and when I told her, she said that she knew exactly where it was and had often wondered if she would be free to just walk in one Saturday. I assured her that she would be more than welcome, and we had prayer together and exchanged numbers.

A few days later, she contacted me, and we began to pray regularly over the phone. During the course of our conversations, I learned that through a set of unfortunate circumstances, this lady had become homeless. Through the promptings of the Holy Spirit, I was led to put into practice the teachings of Isaiah 58. The Lord says that we are to bring the poor that are cast out to our house, so I invited her to come and stay with me while she was in the process of trying to get situated.

She accepted my invitation, and I went and picked her up. Her circumstances had almost driven her to the point of despair. I tried to encourage her each day by demonstrating the love of God. I gave her my bedroom, and I slept in the living room on the sofa. We would have morning and evening devotions together, and she was very grateful because it helped her to understand the Bible better.

This lovely lady stayed with me for six weeks, and through much prayer, the Lord blessed her with her own apartment. But when she left, I was left with bedbugs! My first reaction was anger and hurt. I had extended a helping hand, and this was my repayment? I had to throw away my bed and my sofa and was without any furniture for a month. I slept sitting upright in a folding chair, which resulted in my legs and ankles swelling up like balloons. I went to the emergency room, and after ruling out a blood clot, they told me that it was a circulation problem from sleeping on the chair. I had to wear beige compression stockings every day for a month. They were neither comfortable nor cute!

Our heavenly Father is amazing. He always has a way of speaking to our hearts. One evening I was on the phone with my youngest son Simeon, who was in South Korea at the time. As I was telling him my woes (looking for sympathy), he said, "I understand, Mom, but you know, that's the price you pay whenever you reach out to help someone."

BAM!! His words hit me like a ton of bricks. The following day, the Lord spoke to me through my morning devotions. He said to my spirit, "Is being afflicted with bedbugs too high of a price for you to pay in order to bring someone to Me? I paid an infinite price for *you*. I endured unspeakable agony on Calvary for *you*. Are bedbugs too much for you to endure for My sake?" I fell to my knees in penitence and said, "Please forgive me for complaining, Lord. No, it's not too much for me to endure for You, Lord."

Well, let me tell you how awesome our God is. Not one of the bedbugs bit me. And on top of that, He showed me exactly what to do in order to get rid of every one of them for only twenty-two dollars, when it could have easily cost me several thousand to eradicate them!! The Lord led me to Lowe's Home Improvement, where I was able to purchase some spray and powder, which, when applied, instantly took care of the situation. He also blessed me with a new bed and sofa, much better than I had before. "In the multitude of my anxieties within me, your comforts delight my soul" (Ps. 94:19, NKJV).

My new friend is doing much better now, and we talk often. She told me that I had shown the love of God to her and that she now knows how to have daily devotions from observing me. She gave me a beautiful card that reads,

Have you ever heard of a program called **Amazing Facts?**

"God sent you to be my saving grace, and for this, I will be eternally grateful."

I thank God for this experience and for His tender mercies in allowing me to have the privilege of entering into Christ's sufferings for the salvation of others. It is He "who comforts us in all our tribulation, that we may be able to comfort those who are in any trouble, with the comfort with which we ourselves are comforted by God" (2 Cor. 1:4, NKJV). Praise His holy name!

My friend called me one day and said, "I was flipping through the TV and came across a very interesting channel. Have you ever heard of a program called *Amazing Facts*?" I smiled to myself and thought, "*What an amazing God!*"

21

God ALWAYS Says Yes!

Whenever we pray, there are three possible responses from God: yes, no, or wait. However, I have discovered that there are at least two types of prayers guaranteed to be answered in the affirmative. The first is when you ask for deliverance from sin. It is God's will for you to be set free. That's why Jesus came and died to give you the victory over every besetment. For this reason God will never say no when you pray this prayer. The second is when you pray to be a blessing to someone else. This is also God's will for us because Paul declares that "we are his workmanship, created in Christ Jesus unto good works, which God hath before ordained that we should walk in them" (Eph. 2:10). He also tells us that we should be "zealous of good works" (Titus 2:14).

I stated in my introductory story that I have always been drawn to those who are hurting. I don't know why, but I have an insatiable desire to reach out and soothe people's suffering and heartache. Maybe it's because I know what it feels like to hurt, so it enables me to be sensitive to someone else's pain. That is exactly what happened in the summer of 2017.

It was camp meeting time, and I was a part of the Health Fair, which was sponsored by the Allegheny East Conference for the city of Pottstown, Pennsylvania. I was helping to staff the table for literature distribution when an elderly Caucasian woman approached my table. I welcomed her to the Fair and invited her to take some free literature. As she began to speak, her words quickly turned to tears, and she fell upon my neck weeping profusely.

I mention her ethnicity only to make a point because there's a lesson to be learned. True ministry knows no race, religion, color, or creed. Whoever crosses our path in need of our assistance is our neighbor, and the Lord informs us in Matthew 25:40 that He identifies Himself with His suffering children because He says, "Inasmuch as ye have done it unto one of the least of these my brethren, ye have done it unto me." So I stood there and tenderly held her as she cried.

She was facing some daunting challenges in her life, for which there seemed to be no relief or way of escape. This beautiful child of God was struggling with many health issues and had undergone multiple operations, including two cancer surgeries. She also suffered from depression, chronic stress, and anxiety, which bordered on hypochondria, further complicating her physical ailments. Moreover, there was a straw that was breaking the camel's back. She was a widow, and her house was about to go into foreclosure!

As I helped to wipe away the tears from her eyes, I assured her that God would work everything out for her good. We went over to the prayer booth and offered special prayer and then exchanged numbers. I told her that she could call me at any time. She looked at me tearfully and said, "Do you really mean that? You wouldn't tell me that and not mean it, would you? No one has ever told me that before. No one wants to be bothered with me." I looked her straight in the eye and said, "I really mean it. You can call me anytime." She thanked me again and again and said she felt a little better.

We stayed in contact and have become friends. She took me up on my invitation to call me anytime. Sometimes it would be late at night or early in the morning, but I didn't mind and always gave her the opportunity to vent while I encouraged her in the Lord. I was confident that God would help her because I know my Father. He always roots for the underdog, so to speak. Those who are marginalized and pushed to the outskirts of society, those who are cast aside as worthless and looked upon as a burden are the very ones whom God has a special care for because "The Lord executeth righteousness and judgment for all that are oppressed" (Ps. 103:6). "The Lord also will be a refuge for the oppressed, a refuge in times of trouble" (Ps. 9:9).

I remember once when she had just come home from the hospital after having yet another surgery. It was winter, and there was snow on the ground, and she had no way of picking up her pain medication from the drug store. She called me for prayer, and I cried out to God on her behalf. I told her to watch and see what He would do and to call me back when the blessing came. Later that evening, the phone rang. It was her. Her heart was filled with gratitude and thanksgiving as she related to me what happened.

She said that even though she was in pain, she was going to try and walk to the pharmacy, which was a block or two away. She managed to put on her shoes and make it to the door, but when she opened it, someone she knew was

She owed over $16,000 in taxes with no money to pay.

standing there, getting ready to knock. That person asked her where she was going in such bad weather, and when she explained her dire situation, offered to go and pick up the prescription for her. Praise be to God!! "And they that know thy name will put their trust in thee: for thou, LORD, hast not forsaken them that seek thee" (Ps. 9:10).

As time went on, the deadline approached for the sale of her home, and she had no place to go. She owed over $16,000 in taxes with no money to pay, was sick with worry as the date drew closer, and was faced with the possibility of being homeless. Like the woman with the issue of blood in Luke 8, she had exhausted all her resources and gained no relief. But I had been praying about this situation for a whole year and just believed in my spirit that God would come through for her. I didn't know how or when, but I was certain He wouldn't abandon her when she needed Him the most. We prayed together about a week before the house was to be auctioned off, and I reassured her that the next time we talked, she would have a praise report. Like a little child who takes her friend who is hurt by the hand and comes to mommy confident that she will fix the boo-boo, I sought the Lord earnestly on her behalf during that week and said, "Father, I told her that you would help her. Please honor Your Word. Have mercy upon her, and plead her cause."

Well, July 25, 2018, was the eventful day. I called her that morning, expecting that the Lord had intervened somehow, and He most certainly did!! I could feel her smile through the phone as she told me about her miracle. The Lord used someone who had previously shunned her, telling her not to return to them for help. God gave that individual a change of heart, and they became her advocate. This person did some investigation and filled out the necessary paperwork required to stop the foreclosure and paid the filing fee, which was over $300.

I almost dropped the phone as I raised my hands and voice in thanksgiving and adoration to my Savior. "Bless the Lord, oh my soul: and all that is within me, bless his holy name. Bless the Lord, oh my soul, and forget not all His benefits: Who redeemeth thy life from destruction; who crowneth thee with lovingkindness and tender mercies" (Ps. 103:1–2, 4).

She sent me a beautiful card that reads:

"In life, there are many paths you can take and many people who share the journey, but it's the special people who help you along the way, and it's the most important people who care enough to give of themselves unconditionally. Thank you for being one of those special people."

I hold it as a valuable keepsake because I watched God raise someone up from their bed of languishing—someone

Reader, never underestimate the power of intercessory prayer.

whom life had beaten down to the ground and tossed to and fro like the effects of a hurricane and who no longer had the strength to hold onto His promises for herself.

Reader, never underestimate the power of intercessory prayer, for others can be transported into the very throne room of God on the wings of your faith. "If ye have faith as a grain of mustard seed, ye shall say unto this mountain, Remove hence to yonder place; and it shall remove; and nothing shall be impossible to you" (Matt. 17:20).

22
A Malfunction Miracle

They tell me that confession is good for the soul, so I have one to make. I used to be envious of people who were able to fill their carts up at the supermarket because just about every time I went, I found myself walking up and down the aisles, making mental calculations while counting my change and trying to figure out what I could afford to buy. This constant scenario became frustrating and a bit disheartening to me, especially since I knew that I was faithful in my tithes and offerings.

However, one morning, the Lord spoke to me and revealed just how privileged I really am. I was sitting by my living room window lost in thought and meditation when a little brown sparrow landed on my front lawn. I watched it as it happily scampered here and there across the yard, searching for food. There was no care or anxiety on its tiny brow. At that moment, the Holy Spirit brought to my remembrance these words of Jesus, "Behold the fowls of the air: for they sow not, neither do they reap, nor gather into barns; yet your heavenly Father feedeth them. Are ye not much better than they?" (Matt. 6:26).

For my daily devotional reading, I decided to choose something from one of my favorite authors, Ellen G. White. I picked up *Thoughts from the Mount of Blessing* and began to read the subsection captioned, "Give us this day our daily bread," under the chapter on "The Lord's Prayer." The passage opened my eyes, and I began to understand God's dealings with His children, and that I was in the very place where He wanted me to be. This is what it said:

> If you have renounced self and given yourself to Christ ... everything in the Father's house is for you. All the treasures of God are opened to you, both the world that now is and that which is to come ... The world, with everything in it, is yours so far as it can do you good ... But you are as a child who is not yet placed in control of his inheritance. God does not entrust to you your precious possession,

lest Satan by his wily arts should beguile you, as he did the first pair in Eden. Christ holds it for you, safe beyond the spoiler's reach. Like the child, you shall receive day by day what is required for the day's need. Every day you are to pray, "Give us this day our daily bread." Be not dismayed if you have not sufficient for tomorrow. You have the assurance of His promise, "So shalt thou dwell in the land, and verily thou shalt be fed." David says, "I have been young, and now am old; yet have I not seen the righteous forsaken, nor his seed begging bread" Psalm 37:3, 25 (*Thoughts from the Mount of Blessing*, 1896, p.110).

The reading continued to explain that the God who employed ravens to feed His prophet Elijah in a time of famine would not forget one of His faithful followers.

After reading that passage, the Lord spoke to my spirit and said, "Jean, you are blessed and highly favored. Some people can boast of a providing spouse or a lucrative salary, but your boast is in *Me*, the Creator of heaven and earth. How many people can declare that the God of the universe takes *direct* care of them? No man can claim responsibility for providing for you. Your help comes from *Me* and *Me* alone." Wow! What an epiphany I had that morning. I am living the life that God has intended for me to live—total dependence upon Him! This is why I am so excited about the "malfunction miracle" that I would like to share with you.

On January 3, 2018, I had to travel to Pine Forge, Pennsylvania, concerning my work, which is a roundtrip of 176 miles from my home. I had seven dollars in my pocket and less than half a tank of gas. I prayed and asked my heavenly Father what I should do. I said, "Lord, should I put the seven dollars in on the way there or on the way back?" The Holy Spirit said, "Put it in before you get to Pennsylvania," so I stopped at a gas station on Route 78 and asked the attendant for seven dollars' worth of regular. He took my seven dollars and started the pump before serving another customer. I sat there for a minute, talking to the Lord, and then the thought came to me that it was taking a long time to pump just seven dollars.

As I turned my head and looked at the register, I could not believe my eyes. A little panic set in as it read twenty-five dollars and counting! I quickly blew my horn and called for the attendant who

> *To my utter surprise and delight, the Lord had filled up my gas tank!*

came running over and stopped the pump. I asked him what happened, and he said he didn't know. He said that he preset the pump to dispense seven dollars' worth of gas, but the machine must have malfunctioned. Then he said, "It's not your fault. Just go ahead, and don't even worry about it."

I turned on the ignition, and to my utter surprise and delight, the Lord had filled up my gas tank!! I left there with tears in my eyes and joy in my heart as I thanked my Daddy for taking such good care of me. I felt like I was driving on a cloud. It was such a humbling and awesome experience that I shall always remember. So now, I no longer fret when I don't have enough for tomorrow because I know that all my tomorrows are in God's hands. I am learning to live in the present moment and trust my Father one day at a time.

Oh, and about that supermarket experience? Now, when I see people with their carts filled to the brim, and I look at my items that are budgeted down to the last penny, I walk with a stride in my step and say to myself, "Hmm, if they knew what I know, maybe they'd be a little envious of *me*! Yes, Jean Patrice Good. You truly are blessed beyond measure and highly favored.

Remember, Dear Reader, you may not possess all the worldly advantages that others may have, but know and believe that you have the favor of a loving and caring, covenant-keeping God.

23

The Blessing of a
Ten-Year Prayer

I have often wondered why God likens His love to that of a mother, whether human or animal. He says in Matthew 23:37 when speaking of the inhabitants of Jerusalem, "How often would I have gathered thy children together, even as a hen gathereth her chickens under her wings, and ye would not!" One of the most endearing chapters to me in the whole Bible is Isaiah 49 in its entirety. This chapter is so special because the Lord used it to personally minister to me at one of the lowest points in my life. I have come to the conclusion that the reason why God compares His love to a mother's love is that He knows that there is no greater bond on earth than that of a mother for her child.

I want to bring your attention to a few of the verses. "But Zion said, The Lord hath forsaken me, and my Lord hath forgotten me. Can a woman forget her sucking child, that she should not have compassion on the son of her womb? yea, they may forget, yet will I not forget thee. Behold, I have graven thee upon the palms of my hands; thy walls are continually before me" (verses 14–16)." "Shall the prey be taken from the mighty, or the lawful captive delivered? But thus saith the Lord, Even the captives of the mighty shall be taken away, and the prey of the terrible shall be delivered: for I will contend with him that contendeth with thee, and I will save thy children" (verses 24–25).

I had neither seen nor heard from my eldest son, Ian, in ten years!

I was separated from my two oldest sons for a period of time, which, to me, seemed like an eternity, and it was one of the darkest periods of my life. But I have held on to the promises of Isaiah 49 since 1984. It has encouraged me and kept me going when all seemed lost, and I wanted to give up.

At one point, my heart was heavy with grief and worry because I had neither seen nor heard from my eldest son, Ian, in ten years! I didn't know whether he was dead or alive. His children, his brothers, his friends—no one knew where he was. It was almost as if he had disappeared from the face of the earth. I cried out to God day and night in anguish of spirit, pleading, "Lord, where is my son? Please let me hear from him." The last time I saw him was in the summer of 2008. For ten years, I poured out my heart and soul before my heavenly Father with an earnestness and intensity that only a mother can understand. I can't begin to tell you the number of times that I have engaged in ministry to others during the day, only to come home at night and drown my pillow with tears that flowed freely from a broken heart. However, there's one thing I have discovered about God. He is a promise keeper! This is why His Word means so much to me. He can be trusted to do just what He said He would do. He invites us in Jeremiah 33:3 to "Call unto me, and I will answer thee, and shew thee great and mighty things, which thou knowest not." He said in Luke 18:1 that the parable of the widow and the unjust judge was given to this end, "that men ought always to pray, and not to faint."

After ten long years of persistent prayer, sometimes about to crumble but holding on to God like Jacob through the power of living faith, God finally answered my prayer. On March 8, 2018, at 5:21 p.m., my phone rang. As I looked at the number, I made a mental comment that it was his old area code, but thought that maybe it was one of my grandchildren calling.

When I picked up the phone, heard his voice, and realized that it was actually him, I could hardly believe it was true. I felt like the children of Israel did in Psalm 126:

When the LORD turned again the captivity of Zion, we were like them that dream. Then was our mouth filled with laughter, and our tongue with singing: then said they among the heathen, The LORD hath done great things for them. The LORD hath done great things for us; whereof we are glad. Turn again our captivity, O LORD, as the streams in the south. They that sow in tears shall reap in joy. He that goeth forth and weepeth, bearing precious seed, shall doubtless come again with rejoicing, bringing his sheaves with him.

What a mighty God we serve!! He will fulfill His Word to you no matter how long it takes, so be encouraged if you are praying for your children or loved ones. He has "graven them upon the palms of His hands" (Isa. 49:16), and He *cannot,* He *will not* forget.

24

Blessings Out of Nazareth, NJ?

In 2018, I did Bible work for the Mt. Olivet SDA Church in Camden, New Jersey, under the leadership of Pastor Colby A. Matlock Sr. Two other Bible workers, Kevin Mitchell and Elder Enoch Hopkins, and I labored under some very challenging circumstances.

Camden is a tough place to do ministry. I have worked in some rough areas before, like Baltimore and Newark, so believe me when I tell you, Camden has them beat!

It is a very distressed and impoverished city, and as I entered this mission field, I thought about the passage in John 1:43–46 where Phillip went in search of his friend Nathanael and told him that he had found the Messiah "of whom Moses in the law, and the prophets, did write." Nathanael said, "Can there any good thing come out of Nazareth?" Well, today, Camden would be considered the modern Nazareth, or maybe even worse!

We were giving Bible studies on one side of the street while drugs were being openly sold on the other side. Three people were killed in one day within blocks of each other on some of the very same streets we had worked on earlier that day!

But the Lord woke me up one morning and gave me Acts 18:9–10, "Be not afraid, but speak, and hold not thy peace: For I am with thee, and no man shall set on thee to hurt thee: for I have much people in this city."

> *Judge for yourself whether this is the hand of God or the work of man.*

That's why I like Phillip's response to Nathanael's sarcasm. He simply said, "Come and see." Come and witness for yourself if this be the Messiah or not. And so, Reader, I would like to invite you to journey along with me as I relate this experience of ministering in Camden, and judge for yourself whether this is the hand of God or the work of man.

As we entered the field, we saw the Lord work mightily on our behalf. However, the blessings did not come without opposition. One day, Elder Enoch Hopkins and I encountered a demon-possessed woman. We were doing community surveys door to door, and as we reached a particular home, I began to speak with the young lady who answered the door. Suddenly, we started to hear profanity from inside the house. Soon, another lady came to the door hurling obscenities at us. When she was asked to be quiet, she then ran to the window and continued her vulgar outbursts.

Elder Hopkins and I prayed with the lady who answered the door, and as we left, this demon-possessed woman began to follow us from house to house, cursing and endeavoring to disrupt our work. As we were trying to talk to people, she would yell out, "Go home! What are you doing out here giving people Bible studies?"

I immediately thought about the story in Acts 16, where a young lady who was possessed with a spirit of divination followed Paul and his companions as they were preaching the gospel. So I turned to the woman and in the name of Jesus, rebuked the evil spirit within her. Praise God, she left and began to walk down the street so that we were able to continue with our work.

The Lord did some marvelous things in Camden. I saw Him touch hearts and perform miracles right before my eyes. Kevin Mitchell and I visited a home to follow up on a Bible study that never fully materialized because that wasn't the person whom the Lord had prepared for us. There was a young lady in the home who was listening as Kevin eloquently spoke about the love of God. Her heart was as fertile soil, ready to receive the seed of God's word.

We began studies with her and are trusting that the seed sown will spring up and bear fruit.

One day, while out conducting surveys, I met a nineteen-year-old young man who had wisdom far beyond his years. We began Bible studies with him and his mother, and on one occasion he said to us, "If I'm going to pursue knowledge, I want it to be a knowledge of God. I'm young, and sometimes I get bored, but I don't want to go out into the world. I want to do things God's way." Wow! What a testimony. The Bible study was going great. They were learning things from God's Word that they had never heard before and were enjoying it immensely, which, of course, angered the devil, and so he tried to place a stumbling block in the way. Their pastor told them that they should not be studying with us. It was spiritual warfare from there.

The Bible workers went into serious prayer mode, and the Lord prevailed, even though they discontinued the Bible studies for a while. When the evangelistic meetings were over, we continued to pray for this family, and two months later, I received a text that they wanted to continue with the studies. Praise His name! All power in heaven and on earth is given unto Jesus. I am claiming them for the Lord.

Elder Hopkins and I entered a home where we witnessed the Lord do some miraculous, life-changing things within the space of two months. This lady had some major difficulties with her reading, yet we saw God move her from the basic lessons to complete the advanced lessons and receive her certificate. We arrived one day to discover that, even though she was not familiar with the Bible, she had prayed and tried to find the texts on her own, answering the questions as best she could.

Through much prayer, we marveled at how the Lord finally delivered her mother, who was on oxygen, from chronic nicotine addiction. One day, while we were doing the study, we didn't know that she was upstairs listening. Suddenly, to our surprise, she came running down the stairs, with her oxygen tank on and her Bible in her hand, reading the Scripture that we were on and joining in the Bible study. She, too, completed the advanced lessons and received her certificate, along with another beautiful lady who lived there as well. Our God is an awesome God! He's able to do what no other god can do. Oh, bless His name forevermore.

I met a very lovely lady one day, who, by God's grace, had overcome many insurmountable obstacles and hardships in her life. This woman is a walking miracle, and just like David and Jonathan, it seemed as though our souls were knit together in a bond of friendship as if we had known each other all our lives. I gave her studies, and at the end of the evangelistic

> *There are many today who are nearer the kingdom of God than we suppose.*

series, she was baptized. Praise His holy name. To God be the glory. Great things He has done.

My God truly showed up and showed out in Camden.

There are so many other incredible feats that the Lord performed for us, I wish I had the time to tell it all, but I will end with these quotes from one of my favorite authors, Ellen G. White: "There are many today who are nearer the kingdom of God than we suppose. ... In this dark world of sin, the Lord has many precious jewels to whom He will guide His messengers. ... Everywhere there are those who will take their stand for Christ" (*Review and Herald*, May 12, 1904).

"All over the world men and women are looking wistfully to heaven. Prayers and tears and inquiries go up from souls longing for light, for grace, for the Holy Spirit. Many are on the verge of the kingdom, waiting only to be gathered in" (*Acts of the Apostles*, p. 109).

Yes, my friend. Jesus knew best when He said in John 4:35, "Say not ye, There are yet four months, and then cometh harvest? behold, I say unto you, Lift up your eyes, and look on the fields; for they are white already to harvest."

I don't know what kind of fruit they had in the Nazareth of Jesus' day, but this I do know. The fruit in Nazareth, New Jersey, is surely ripe for the picking.

25

A Blessing at Last

One afternoon in September 2018, I was out knocking on doors in Piscataway, New Jersey. It was very cold that day, and I knew that I could not stay outside for long, so I decided to try and brave the elements for one hour. After about forty-five minutes and thirty doors later, with hardly a positive response, I was done! My feet were cold, my hands were freezing, and I just felt like a giant icicle.

I said, "Okay, Lord. This is it. I'm going home." I looked at my watch, and it was 2:50. As I turned to leave, the Lord responded and said, "Wait a minute; not so fast. You said you were going to work for an hour. You have ten minutes left. Just go a little farther, and knock on a few more doors."

By God's grace, I mustered up the courage to keep going. I was working in an apartment complex, and when I

> *By God's grace, I mustered up the courage to keep going.*

reached the last door in that particular section, a gentleman opened the door and greeted me kindly. I explained to him that I was doing missionary work in the community and would like to leave some literature with him. He purchased a *Steps to Christ* and asked me to what church I belonged. I replied that I was a Seventh-day Adventist. I asked him where he worshiped, and he told me that he was, in fact, a pastor of another denomination.

Then he looked at me and said, "So why are you a Seventh-day Adventist?" I responded, "Because I believe and obey God's Word found in Exodus 20:8–11, where He says, *"Remember the Sabbath day to keep it holy."* I had prayer with him, and he stepped out onto the porch to continue our conversation.

He questioned me again and said, "So how long have you been a Seventh-day Adventist, and what made you join the church?" I told him since 1980, but then added that it really wasn't about me being a Seventh-day Adventist, but what was more important was my personal relationship with Jesus Christ.

This pastor's response blew me away! He said, "I'm so glad you said that. I'm actually convicted about the Sabbath. I read it in the Bible and believe that the seventh day is the Sabbath, but what I don't like about Seventh-day Adventists is that whenever you talk to them, they usually wind up putting the Sabbath before their relationship with Christ. I know several people who keep the Sabbath, but you are the first Seventh-day Adventist that I have talked to who has actually put their relationship with Jesus before the Sabbath." Wow! His words resounded in my ears like a megaphone. I sat there on his porch, saying to myself, "Lord, have mercy."

He told me that he had been fasting and praying, seeking guidance from God regarding the Sabbath, and had stopped working on Saturdays. He would stay home and read his Bible. But one day, the Holy Spirit said to him, "It's good that you're praying and reading your Bible, but this is not what keeping the Sabbath is all about. You've got to be ministering to people." I listened in awe at the mighty power of God working in this man's life. I offered him a copy of *The Great Controversy,* which he accepted, and this time *he* prayed for me and thanked me for the work that I was doing in the community and for knocking on his door that day.

As I left and walked back to my car, the only part of my body that wasn't chilled was my heart. It had been kept warm by the fire of the Holy Spirit, who helped me to persevere in my search for souls and had done for me in ten minutes what I couldn't accomplish in an hour. "They that sow in tears shall reap in joy. He that goeth forth and weepeth, bearing precious seed, shall doubtless come again with rejoicing, bringing his sheaves with him" (Psalm 126:5–6).

26

The Miracle of the Locked Door

I stated in one of my earlier chapters that I've discovered at least two prayers that God will always answer in the affirmative. One is when we ask for deliverance from sin, and the other is when we ask to be a blessing to someone else. It was June 4, 2019, my friend Carrian Williams' birthday. She'd been through so much hurt and disappointment in life (her story is told in chapter 18), that I just wanted to surprise her with some special gifts that I had purchased.

However, I was in Camden, New Jersey, at the time, doing some Bible work, so I decided to drive back home early that morning to pick up the gifts and drop them off. When I arrived home, to my dismay, my house keys were nowhere to be found. After searching my car and purse diligently, I finally came to the unwanted conclusion that I had done the unthinkable. I had left my keys in Camden, which is an hour and a half away!

What do I do now? Well, I prayed and asked for God's help. My neighbor downstairs opened the front door for me, as I explained to her my dilemma. Then we went upstairs to my apartment and began trying different things. A credit card didn't work; a knife, same result. I tried my neighbor's front door key. It fit the lock, but wouldn't turn it. After several minutes of trying different things to no avail, my neighbor went back downstairs to see what else she could come up with.

> *As soon as I finished praying, to my amazement, I felt the lock turn without the key moving, and my door opened up!*

I stood there for a few minutes, fiddling with the key in the lock. By this time, I was at my wits' end. I knew that I had to get back down to Camden, yet I desperately wanted to bless my friend. Standing there with my hand on the key, I prayed this prayer: "Lord, I need you to send an angel to open this door."

As soon as I finished praying, to my amazement, I felt the lock turn without the key moving, and my door opened up!!! I was in shock! I lifted my hands and voice in praise and thanksgiving to my God. I hurried inside and fell to my knees, letting Him know how grateful I was for His miraculous intervention. The same God who sent His angel to shut the lions' mouths for Daniel, had commissioned an angel to open the door for Jean Good. Hallelujah! Praise God. He is no respecter of persons. What He's done for others, He will do for you and me, if we believe.

When Carrian received her birthday surprise, she was elated. She told me that it was the best birthday she had ever had and that I had really made her day. As I drove back to Camden, I contemplated the goodness of God and how He'll go to any lengths to brighten up your day and make you a blessing, even if it means sending an angel from heaven to unlock a door.

27

That's Not How
My Story Ends

Jean Patrice Good
A Celebration of Life
Sunrise–Sunset
October 31, 1958–October 4, 2018

Yes, it's true! October 4, 2018, at 7:30 p.m., could
very well have been the end of my story. On this
eventful day, a policeman drew his gun on me,

aimed, and was ready to fire, but my God said *no*, for "the angel of the Lord encampeth round about them that fear Him, and delivereth them" (Ps. 34:7).

When we pray to be a blessing to others, we never know by what means God will choose to answer our prayers. I had been praying for my neighbor and her boyfriend that the Lord would give me an opportunity to witness to them. It always seems easier to approach people who don't know you than those who see you every day. But I thank the Lord that everywhere I have lived, whether Baltimore or New Jersey, He has given me the courage to witness in my neighborhood.

My neighbor and I had become friends, and I knew that my lifestyle was a living testimony, but I wanted to engage her about the love of God and to accept Him as her personal Savior. Christmas of 2017, I gave her and her boyfriend a copy of *Peace Above the Storm*, which is just a larger, illustrated version of the book *Steps to Christ*, and outlines how to know God better. She told me that she had read a little of the book, but then it got misplaced.

Ten months later, on October 4, my neighbor and her boyfriend got into a big fight, which resulted in the police and ambulance being called. I heard her crying downstairs, and I said, "Lord, what can I do to help her?" As I opened my door and stepped out into the hallway, to my surprise, two police officers were standing at the bottom of my stairs, one with his gun aimed at me in a shooting stance!!

God is so good!! During this incident, I kept amazingly calm. I did not panic or make any sudden moves. The news is filled with tragic stories of unarmed people being shot and killed by law enforcement officers who pull the trigger first and ask questions later. But for the grace of God, this could have resulted in a very different outcome for me.

When he realized the magnitude of what could have happened, the policeman who drew his gun put it back into the holster, and shook his head with a sigh of relief, as if to say, "Oh, my God! I almost shot this lady." Both officers apologized profusely and asked for my forgiveness.

I mentioned earlier that at the moment this occurred, there was no fear. But after it was all over, and for several days to follow, I was quite shaken by the reality of what had taken place, and the thought that my children could have been making funeral arrangements for me right then.

Thankfully, I was still able to go down that evening and minister to my neighbor. The next day, she came up to see me, and when she learned what had transpired between the police and me, she was sorrowful and heartbroken. Her heart was now softened and subdued, and I was able to speak to her about the love of God and give her words of encouragement that dropped like seeds into fertile soil. She asked me if I would pray with her, and as we prayed together, in my heart, I thanked the Lord for once again allowing me the privilege and opportunity to be of service. I gave her another copy of *Steps to Christ,* which she has been reading.

Since this harrowing experience, we have grown a little closer. She thanked me for helping her and told me that my prayers mean the world to her. Thank You, Jesus. Through the seeds that have been sown, imperceptible as they may be, I believe that God is going to do a new thing in her life.

And as for me? Well, I have a feeling that God is not through with me, either. There are still some more chapters

What does God want to accomplish in your life?

that He wants to write in my life because, after all, this isn't how my story ends ... to be continued.

What about you, Reader? What does God want to accomplish in your life? I pray that as you seek His guidance, your heart and mind will become as blank paper, ready to receive the ink marks of His Spirit, as your own life story continues to unfold.

Reviews

"A stimulating and faith-provoking read. Jean Good narrates many of her moving encounters on the frontline of gospel ministry and in her own personal experiences. This book captures several accounts I've heard her recount at our monthly pastors' area meeting in Northern New Jersey. The Lord has been doing a mighty work through her across several cities in this part of the state. She frequents some of the most dangerous streets in the state, often with no human companion or bodyguard. This simple, humble lady of peace goes to war every day with an assurance that angels still provide the best security service on the planet."

—Richard Campbell PhD LPC, Pastor of First Seventh-day Adventist Church of Paterson, NJ.

"After reading this collection, I was reminded of what I've always known, even as a young boy. I came away with the feeling that the author, my mother, is a woman of strength; strength developed and forged out of the many lemons that life sometimes throws. As I read, I saw her story merging with the stories of the ancient Bible writers of old: of Daniel in the lion's den, of Jacob and his midnight fight with the Almighty, and, indeed, of the little shepherd boy David as he took on the big-toothed, ugly-faced, stank-breathed Goliath. It's an old story, one that's been stitched together from century to century. A story that speaks of God's unwavering faithfulness."

—Simeon Good, SGT United States Army, one of the author's sons.

Bibliography

White, Ellen G. "Into Clearer Light," *Review and Herald*, May 12, 1904.

White, Ellen G. *The Ministry of Healing.* Mountain View, CA: Pacific Press Publishing Association, 1905.

White, Ellen G. *Thoughts from the Mount of Blessing.* Mountain View, CA: Pacific Press Publishing Association, 1896.

TEACH Services, Inc.
P U B L I S H I N G

We invite you to view the complete
selection of titles we publish at:
www.TEACHServices.com

We encourage you to write us
with your thoughts about this,
or any other book we publish at:
info@TEACHServices.com

TEACH Services' titles may be purchased in
bulk quantities for educational, fund-raising,
business, or promotional use.
bulksales@TEACHServices.com

Finally, if you are interested in seeing
your own book in print, please contact us at:
publishing@TEACHServices.com
We are happy to review your manuscript at no charge.